RIGGED

*Exposing the Largest
Financial Fraud in History*

Stuart Englert

Printed in the United States of America
Fourth Edition: October 2020
Cover photo: PM Imagery

Library of Congress Cataloging-in-Publication Data

Englert, Stuart
Rigged—Exposing the Largest Financial Fraud in
History / Stuart Englert

Summary: "The federal government and its banking
accomplices for decades have colluded to suppress
gold and silver prices to defend the U.S. dollar.
Documentary evidence reveals precious metals markets
have been manipulated to mask the dollar's declining
value and maintain its role as the world's reserve
currency."

ISBN: 9781651405208 (paperback) :
1. —Financial—United States 2. Fraud—United States
3. Gold—United States 4. Silver—United States 5.
Precious Metals—United States 6. Price—United States
7. Manipulation—United States 8. Suppression—
United States 9. Dollar—United States

Dedicated to free markets and sound money.

Acknowledgments

Special thanks to the Gold Anti-Trust Action Committee and the many gold and silver analysts, researchers and scholars who diligently document and expose market manipulation and precious metals price suppression.

"Gold is money, and nothing else."

—J.P. Morgan
December 19, 1912

"There are no markets anymore, just interventions."
—Chris Powell, secretary/treasurer of the
Gold Anti-Trust Action Committee (GATA)
April 18, 2008

Introduction

The largest financial fraud in history wasn't Enron's colossal accounting crimes, Bernie Madoff's record-setting Ponzi scheme or the Libor scandal, in which some of the world's biggest banks conspired to profit by manipulating interest rates.

No, the largest financial fraud in history is one most Americans know little to nothing about. It isn't mentioned by politicians, reported on the nightly news or discussed by coworkers during lunch break.

The biggest fraud in history is a financial scheme perpetrated by the U.S. government and its banking accomplices. Over the last century, they've used coercion, deception and market manipulation to convince Americans the U.S. dollar is as good as gold and silver.

The truth is, it's not.

1

Defending the Dollar

Defending the dollar is paramount to the U.S. government and the American way of life. It's far more important than securing the nation's borders or stopping terrorists from entering the country. It's more important than reducing the nation's massive trade deficit and burgeoning $27 trillion national debt.

Yet, most Americans are unaware of the significance of the dollar's status as the world's dominant currency. Most of us go about our daily lives never considering the vital role the money in our pockets and purses plays on the world stage.

We should.

If the dollar loses its status as the top currency in global trade, Americans will lose the enormous privilege of living beyond their means. The United States will lose its ability to run massive trade deficits and accumulate enormous debt. It will lose its sole superpower status and the ability to bankroll its mighty military, deployed around the world to subdue economic adversaries and destroy challengers to the monetary world order.

The world as we know it will change. Our lives will change.

U.S. politicians seldom discuss the countless benefits of issuing the world's preeminent currency. They seldom speak publicly about the dollar or its diminishing status as a global asset. Presumably, they don't want to undermine confidence in the dollar or draw attention to the sensitive national—and economic—security issue.

But behind closed doors, government and banking officials strategize and scheme to keep the U.S. dollar top dog. They impose economic sanctions and tariffs against rival nations, initiate and fund wars under the guise of protecting democracy, and manipulate financial markets to ensure the dollar remains the world's reserve currency.

The purpose of this book is to reveal how the federal government and its banking collaborators rig gold and silver prices to defend the U.S. dollar.

Hoarded & Feared

The federal government has a love-hate relationship with precious metals. On one hand, the U.S. Treasury claims to hold 8,133 metric tons of gold—the largest hoard in the world—as a financial asset. On the other hand, gold and silver are feared because they compete with—and pose a threat to—the U.S. dollar.

Despite conflicting sentiments, precious metals are trusted and time-tested money. Gold and silver have been used as metallic mediums of exchange since the 7th century B.C. That's when the first gold and silver coins were minted in the Kingdom of Lydia, in modern western Turkey.

Gold and silver were money 2,300 years before the United States was conceived and 550 years before the birth of Jesus Christ. Gold and silver are referenced in the Bible—both favorably and unfavorably—more than 700 times. Gold and silver are the only kind of money mentioned in the U.S. Constitution, the supreme law of the land. Gold was accepted and used as money in the United States until 1933. The nation's coinage contained silver until the 1960s and '70s.

Still, some in the government and banking institutions fear gold and silver because they rival the U.S. dollar. Gold and silver prices also act as a barometer on the value of government-issued paper and digital currency. Rising precious metal prices indicate the U.S. dollar is losing value. A declining dollar erodes public confidence and poses a threat to the nation's economic stability and security.

To defend the dollar, government and banking officials intervene in currency and precious metals markets. They suppress gold and silver prices. Price suppression protects the U.S. dollar while banks profit by trading and manipulating precious metals.

Age-Old Deception

Money manipulation is an age-old deception used to retain political and economic power. Corrupt kings and authoritarian regimes have debased coins and devalued currencies since ancient times.

In modern times, governments, central banks and bullion banks continue the role of currency manipulators, dictating the price of gold, silver and paper money through both lawful and unlawful means. Bullion bankers and traders in London, England, began "fixing"—or setting—the gold price in 1919. At the time, the price in New York was $19.39 a troy ounce. The London Gold Fix continues today and trading on the London bullion market is used to rig precious metal prices.

In the last century, the U.S. government hoodwinked its citizens by removing gold and silver from the monetary system and devaluing its paper currency. During the Great Depression, Americans hoarded gold because they didn't trust the banks, so the government forced them to hand over their gold.

On April 5, 1933, President Franklin D. Roosevelt issued an executive order requiring citizens to surrender their gold coins, bars and certificates to the Federal Reserve banks by May 1. In exchange, they received $20.67 in paper currency for each troy ounce. Violators faced up to a $10,000 fine and/or 10 years in prison.1 Though contrary to the Constitution, the seizure effectively abolished gold as legal tender in the United States.

"Behind government currency we have, in addition to the promise to pay, a reserve of gold and a small reserve of silver, neither of them anything like the total amount of the currency," President Roosevelt said during a fireside chat recorded on May 7, 1933.2

Roosevelt's admission revealed insufficient gold and silver stocks to back the nation's paper currency. It also confirmed the government's involvement in a scheme to deceive bank depositors and the general public. The Federal Reserve, the nation's central bank, and the U.S. Treasury didn't have enough metal to cover all the banknotes and gold certificates in circulation—or the paper currency they wanted to issue—so the government outlawed gold as money in the United States. Amid the financial crisis, the move avoided unraveling of the fraudulent monetary scheme.

Following passage of the Gold Reserve Act of 1934,3 President Roosevelt raised the gold price to $35 an ounce. The action devalued the dollar, effectively stealing 69 percent in purchasing power from law-abiding citizens who 10 months earlier were coerced to exchange their gold for dollars. In hopes of ending the Great Depression, loyal and trusting Americans became victims of a government-sanctioned gold heist and currency depreciation.

With $2 billion in profit earned from an estimated 4,340 metric tons of surrendered gold, the U.S. Treasury established the Exchange Stabilization Fund (ESF). To this day, the fund is used to manipulate currency and precious metals markets.

Done with its gold caper, the U.S. government turned to silver. On June 19, 1934, Congress passed the Silver Purchase Act, allowing President Roosevelt to nationalize domestic silver stocks and mine production.4 Two months later, Roosevelt issued an executive order limiting silver ownership, imposing a government-mandated silver price and tax, and requiring non-monetary silver stocks to be delivered to the U.S. Mint to be stored or made into coins. Subjugation of precious metals was nearly complete.

The final blow on the domestic front came in the 1960s and '70s. That's when the federal government reduced—and ultimately eliminated—the silver content of its coinage and halted exchange of dollars for silver. Facing a silver shortage, the U.S. Treasury stopped issuing silver dimes and quarters in 1964, and by 1968 redemption of silver certificates ceased. In 1976, the last silver-containing Eisenhower dollar was minted.

"If we had not done so, we would have risked chronic coin shortages in the very near future," President Lyndon Johnson told Congress before signing the Coinage Act of 1965.[5]

Johnson added: "If anybody has any idea of hoarding our silver coins, let me say this. [The] Treasury has a lot of silver on hand, and it can be, and will be used to keep the price of silver in line with its value in our present silver coin[s]. There will be no profit in holding them out of circulation for the value of their silver content."[6]

Not only did Johnson's remarks reveal the government's intention to suppress the silver price, in retrospect he was wrong about hoarding silver coins. Based on today's price of $24 an ounce, the silver in a 1964 Roosevelt dime is worth $1.74; a 1964 Washington quarter, $4.35; and a 1964 Kennedy half-dollar, $8.70.

With precious metals no longer money in the United States, a final obstacle remained: elimination of gold in foreign exchange. Before abandoning the international gold standard, however, an attempt was made to maintain gold at $35 an ounce.

In 1961, the Federal Reserve and seven European central banks formed the London Gold Pool. Combining 240 metric tons of gold, the banks traded the metal in the London market to defend the price set by Allied nations toward the end of World War II. While the effort worked for a while, ultimately it failed over fears the United States couldn't meet its financial obligations.

Faith in the U.S. dollar waned as the nation's money supply, trade imbalances and budget deficits grew. France withdrew from the London Gold Pool in 1967 and began redeeming dollars for gold. The Netherlands also exchanged dollars for gold. After the United Kingdom devalued its currency, further boosting gold demand, the London Gold Pool collapsed in 1968. Without coordinated central bank sales, the gold price rose, surpassing $40 an ounce for the first time.

Fearing depletion of the nation's gold holdings, President Richard Nixon in 1971 halted the exchange of dollars for gold with foreign nations.

"I have directed [Treasury] Secretary [John] Connally to suspend temporarily the convertibility of the dollar into gold or other reserve assets except in amounts and conditions determined to be in the interest of monetary stability and in the best interests of the United States," Nixon said in a televised address on Aug. 15, 1971.[7]

The decision to sever the link between the dollar and gold became permanent, ensuring perpetual currency debasement and price inflation. Nixon devalued the dollar twice before resigning from office in 1974 as the gold price exceeded $150 an ounce.

With the dollar decoupled from gold, only public confidence and military might backed the world's reserve currency, requiring the U.S. government and banks to renew efforts to contain the price of precious metals and retain dollar supremacy.

While efforts to suppress gold and silver prices are ongoing, a paradigm shift is underway. The pendulum reversed course after President Gerald Ford signed a law repealing the prohibition on private gold ownership in 1974.[8] Americans once again could legally purchase, possess and sell the precious metal. The problem was gold coins were scarce due to the government's seizure 40 years earlier, which only permitted Americans to retain up to 5 ounces of gold and rare collectable coins.

Availability increased after President Ronald Reagan signed the Gold Bullion Coin and Liberty Coin acts of 1985, legalizing the issuance of constitutional money.[9,10] The next year, the U.S. Mint began issuing 1-ounce gold and silver American Eagle coins.

While hundreds of millions of silver and gold coins have been struck and sold since 1986, they're not used as currency since their metal value far exceeds their face value of $1 and $50, respectively. Moreover, most Americans don't own precious metals and few are aware of today's silver and gold prices.

Despite rising precious metal prices over the last 100 years, their value has not kept pace with the creation of trillions of dollars of paper and digital currency and credit. This not only indicates that gold and silver prices are suppressed, it also helps explain why.

When precious metal prices rise and the dollar declines in value, more Americans—and foreign nations—exchange dollars for gold and silver, undermining the national currency. If precious metals demand exceeds supply, prices will spiral out of control, setting the stage for collapse of the dollar and its century-long reign as the world's reserve currency. That's why the U.S. government fears gold and silver, and suppresses their prices with the help of central and bullion banks, which deal in precious metals.

Abundance of Evidence

While presidential orders and congressional acts reveal efforts to manipulate the currency and defend the dollar, an abundance of other evidence confirms motives and methods to suppress gold and silver prices.

Dozens of documents dating back decades prove both overt and covert measures to thwart and circumvent free markets in precious metals. Some of the evidence is circumstantial, but collectively audio transcripts, public testimony and written records confirm gold sales, leases and swaps are used to protect the nation's currency and intervene in financial markets.

A Federal Reserve memorandum dated April 5, 1961, offers insight into the motive and methods. Marked "Confidential," the memo cites gold holdings in the U.S. Treasury's Exchange Stabilization Fund and details a plan to intervene in foreign exchange markets. The plan suggests ways to conceal or obscure currency intervention to support the dollar.

"Operations could under present conditions be masked to some extent by careful supervision of the account and a selective use of 'swaps,'" concludes the proposal, implying the exchange of gold for currency or vice versa.

Titled "U.S. Foreign Exchange Operations: Needs and Methods," the document was discovered among the papers of William McChesney Martin Jr., chairman of the Federal Reserve from 1951 to 1970. It's part of the Missouri Historical Society's archives.11

In his autobiographical recollections, former Federal Reserve Chairman Paul Volcker expressed regret that central banks didn't intervene in the gold market in 1973 when the dollar was devalued 10 percent and the gold price rose above $100 an ounce.

"Joint intervention in gold sales to prevent a steep rise in the price of gold, however, was not undertaken. That was a mistake," Volcker asserted in his memoirs, excerpts of which were published in *The Nikkei Weekly* in Japan on Nov. 15, 2004.12

In his 1992 book, "Changing Fortunes: The World's Money and the Threat to American Leadership," Volcker, who served as Federal Reserve chairman from 1979 to 1987, said "a nation's [currency] exchange rate is the single most important price in the economy."13 That statement affirms why the gold price is suppressed. In a free market, gold competes with and reveals the declining value of the dollar.

When Volcker served as undersecretary of the Treasury for international affairs during the Nixon administration, he supported ending redemption of dollars for gold. He considered the decision "the single most important event of his career," author William L. Silber wrote in his 2012 book "Volcker: The Triumph of Persistence."[14]

In a 2012 note to freelance journalist Lar Schall, Volcker denied any knowledge of U.S. intervention in the gold market in the previous 40 years. Three years later, however, he acknowledged gold was his adversary when he headed the Federal Reserve. After the gold price spiked to a record $850 an ounce in 1980, Volcker pushed interest rates to 20 percent to battle double-digit price inflation.

"Gold was the enemy to me because that was a speculative vehicle while I was trying to hold the system together. [The speculators] were on the other side," Volcker remarked during a meeting of the Committee for Monetary Research and Education at the University Club in New York on March 25, 2015.[15]

Speculators, investors and some European central bankers bought gold in the 1960s and 1970s to increase earnings and preserve wealth rather than relying solely on the depreciating U.S. dollar.

The late Dutch prime minister, treasurer and banking official Jelle Zijlstra was among them. Zijlstra was at the helm of the Netherlands central bank when the London Gold Pool collapsed in 1968. With declining faith in the U.S. government's ability to meet its financial obligations, the bank exchanged some of its dollar holdings for gold.

Volcker, Treasury undersecretary at the time, urged Zijlstra against the move during a visit to the Netherlands in 1971, according to the 1979 book "Dr. Jelle Zijlstra, Conversations and Writings."

"You are rocking the boat," Volcker is quoted as saying.

"If the boat is rocking because we present $250 million for conversion into gold or something that can be considered an equal asset, then the boat *has* already perished," Zijlstra replied.16

Zijlstra later confirmed gold price suppression. "Gold is artificially kept at a far too low price,'" he wrote in his 1992 memoirs *"Per Slot Van Rekening"* or "The Final Settlement."17

While Zijlstra didn't specify how the price is restrained, he referred to gold as the sun in the "monetary cosmos." In other words, all national currencies ultimately revolve around gold regardless of central bank interventions.

Little wonder Volcker and other U.S. officials wanted gold removed from the global monetary system. They had difficulty controlling foreign central banks and the metal's price, particularly after U.S. gold holdings declined by 12,000 tons in the 1960s and '70s.

During a U.S. State Department meeting on April 25, 1974, Secretary of State Henry Kissinger asked: "Why is it against our interest to have gold in the [international monetary] system?"

"It's against our interest to have gold in the system because for it to remain there it would result in it being evaluated periodically," replied Thomas O. Enders, assistant undersecretary of state for economic and business affairs. "Although we have still some substantial gold holdings—about $11 billion—a larger part of the official gold in the world is concentrated in Western Europe. This gives them the dominant position in world [gold] reserves and the dominant means of creating [currency] reserves. We've been trying to get away from that into a system in which we can control . . ."

In other words, those who hold the most gold make the rules, along with the authority to issue the world's dominant currency and set the gold price.

During the State Department meeting, attendees discussed strategies to keep France, the Netherlands and other European countries from increasing the gold price. Enders suggested selling gold to smash the price and obliterate its role as money.

"I think we should look very hard then, Ken [Rush, deputy secretary of state], at very substantial sales of gold—U.S. gold on the market—to raid the gold market once and for all," he said.

Later in the conversation, Kissinger offered to speak with Federal Reserve Chairman Arthur Burns about the matter. "The gold market is generally in cahoots with Arthur Burns," he said, suggesting the central banker was personally engaged in gold price manipulation.[18]

A declassified letter, dated June 3, 1975, confirms Burns' clandestine meddling in the gold market. "I have a secret understanding in writing with the Bundesbank [German central bank], concurred in by Mr. [Helmut] Schmidt [West Germany's chancellor at the time] that Germany will not buy gold, either from the market or from another government, at a price above the official price of $42.22 per ounce," Burns wrote to President Ford.

Burns added: "I am convinced that by far the best position for us to take at this time is to resist arrangements that provide wide latitude for central banks and governments to purchase gold at a market-related price."[19] The undeniable goal was price suppression.

Former U.S. Treasury Secretary Lawrence Summers is among officials who provided a motive for the federal government to rig the gold price. He did so when he was an economics professor at Harvard University in the 1980s. A paper written by Summers and University of Michigan economics professor Robert Barsky cited gold's influence on currencies, interest rates and government bond prices.

"Data from recent years indicate that changes in long-term real interest rates are indeed associated with movements in the relative price of gold in the opposite direction and that this effect is a dominant feature of gold price fluctuations," contend the authors of the paper, published in the *Journal of Political Economy* in 1988.

Titled "Gibson's Paradox and the Gold Standard," the paper implies governments can achieve lower interest rates and strengthen government bond prices by controlling the gold price. Since the Federal Reserve sets interest rates and the U.S. Treasury issues government bonds, both have a reason to control the price of gold.

"The willingness to hold the stock of gold depends on the rate of return available on alternative assets," the paper concludes. "We assume that the alternative assets are physical capital and bonds, both earning a real return."[20]

In other words, if investors can earn more money on bank deposits and bond yields, they won't buy and hoard gold, which offers no interest or rate of return, diminishing gold as a competitor with the U.S. dollar and debt instruments.

Summers served as U.S. Treasury secretary from 1999 to 2001 after stints as the department's undersecretary for international affairs and deputy secretary. He also served as director of the National Economic Council from 2009 to 2010.

While the motive for suppressing precious metals is obvious, the methods are not so clear-cut. The complexity of the behind-the-scenes scheme, particularly the financial tools and tricks used by manipulators, make the plot difficult—if not impossible—for casual observers to follow. Still, astute and inquisitive researchers have exposed the monetary illusion, shedding light on the maneuvers and mechanisms used to rig gold and silver prices.

Market Manipulations

Sales, swaps and leases—along with financial derivatives—are the primary methods and mechanisms used to manipulate the gold and silver markets.

The most direct way to suppress precious metal prices is to flood the market with gold and silver. The chief constraint to this method is exhaustion of supply by willing sellers, especially when demand is strong.

But that didn't stop the United States and International Monetary Fund (IMF) from trying after the London Gold Pool collapsed in 1968. Between 1970 and 1980, the United States and IMF sold more than 2,300 tons of gold. The effort to commandeer the market failed, however, as demand outpaced supply.

Another attempt to subdue the gold price was made in 1999 with adoption of the Washington Gold Agreement, later called the Central Bank Gold Agreement. Signed by 15 European central banks during an IMF meeting in Washington, D.C., the agreement was renewed in 2004, 2009 and 2014, and expanded to include six other central banks.21 The stated—and contradictory—goal of the accord, which expired in 2019, was to limit dishoarding that could unsettle the gold market.

Under the agreement, European central banks and the IMF sold some 4,000 tons of gold, about 12 percent of world reserves. The Bank of England auctioned off 395 tons—half of the United Kingdom's gold reserves— from 1999 to 2002. Other European central banks and the IMF unloaded the remainder. Once again the effort failed to contain the gold price, which climbed to $1,900 an ounce in 2011, a new high at the time. Gold sales, however, may have prevented the price from rising even higher during the financial crisis of 2007 and 2008 when massive amounts of money were injected into the global financial system.

While dishoarding proved inadequate to subjugate gold, banks and traders exploit other market mechanisms to manipulate precious metals. Since the 1970s, they've used financial instruments called derivatives to suppress gold and silver prices. Derivatives allow traders to fabricate tons of imaginary metal. The imaginary metal exists only digitally or on paper, not in physical form, and often is referred to as "paper gold."

By leasing and swapping physical metal, banks can generate an enormous supply of "paper gold." This imaginary metal is traded in futures, options and forwards contracts in the precious metals markets. Gold futures trading began on the Commodity Exchange Inc. (COMEX) in New York on Dec. 31, 1974, which coincided with the repeal of a 41-year ban on private ownership of gold by U.S. citizens. A telegram sent to the U.S. Secretary of State from the U.S. Embassy in London, England, on Dec. 10, 1974, reveals the importance of gold sales and futures trading. In the telegram, presumably written by the embassy's Deputy Chief Ronald Spiers, London gold dealers are described as praising the announced sale of 2 million ounces of U.S. gold and predicting deregulation of—and volatility in—the futures market would reduce demand for physical metal.

"Each of the dealers expressed the belief that the futures market would be of significant proportion and physical trading would be miniscule by comparison," reads the cable released by WikiLeaks. "Also expressed was the expectation that large volume futures dealing would create a highly volatile market. In turn, the volatile price movements would diminish the initial demand for physical holdings and most likely negate long-term hoarding by U.S. citizens."[22]

Translation: Financial markets can be used to reduce gold demand and price fluctuations will discourage people from buying or holding the metal.

Leasing also is used to restrain precious metals. Federal Reserve Chairman Alan Greenspan testified about gold leasing in 1998. He told Congress central banks were prepared to lease gold to curtail its price. Speaking in his trademark convoluted language, he also revealed how gold supplies are expanded via derivatives trading.

"Nor can private counterparties restrict supplies of gold, another commodity whose derivatives are often traded over-the-counter, where central banks stand ready to lease gold in increasing quantities should the price rise," said Greenspan, testifying before Congress on July 24, 1998.[23]

During his testimony, Greenspan opposed regulation of financial derivatives, which allow traders to bet on the future price of gold and silver without possessing or exchanging any metal. He also alluded to the seemingly endless supply of metal available with financial derivatives.

"It is not possible to corner a market for financial futures where the underlying asset or its equivalent is in essentially unlimited supply," said Greenspan, who headed the nation's central bank from 1987 to 2006.

Since most gold and silver futures contracts traded on the COMEX are settled in cash rather than metal, derivatives are the primary means to suppress prices. The unregulated financial devices—and their accompanying make-believe metal—are traded in such large quantities that they dwarf the physical gold and silver market.

Precious metals market expert Jeffrey Christian, managing director of CPM Group, divulged the extent of derivatives trading during a Commodity Futures Trading Commission (CFTC) hearing on March 25, 2010. He acknowledged precious metals "trade in the multiples of a hundred times the underlying physical [metal] . . ."[24]

More imaginary gold and silver is traded in a few days than is mined in an entire year. Such large-scale trading is at the heart of the price suppression scheme. The scheme creates an illusion of supply, allowing precious metal prices to be manipulated lower even if physical demand rises.

An article in *Precious Metal Investor* describes how bullion banks and dealers capitalize on—and pyramid—their precious metal trades to influence prices.

"The way in which banks monetize their gold and silver positions, using them as collateral for subsequent trades, is integral to understanding what has been driving gold and silver prices over the past several years," reads an excerpt from "Bullion Banking Explained," published in CPM Group's February 2000 newsletter.

The newsletter also details massive trading volume in the major metals markets, including the London Bullion Market Association (LBMA) exchange, where derivatives also dictate gold and silver prices.

"With the start of the London Bullion Market Association's release of monthly trading data, the market has become aware that 100 times more gold and silver trade hands each year, just in the major markets, than is produced or used. Some market participants have wondered aloud how 10 billion ounces of gold could trade via the major markets each year, compared to 120 million ounces of total supply and demand, while roughly 100 billion ounces of silver change hands, compared to around 628 million ounces of new supply," the newsletter states.[25]

Twenty years later, trading volume continues to eclipse physical supply, precious metal derivatives proliferate into the billions of dollars, and some market participants and analysts wonder how large the derivatives bubble can grow before it pops.

Derivatives are used in tandem with gold leases and swaps to expand the supply of imaginary metal. Leases and swaps also are used to inject physical metal into the market. While details about lease and swap agreements are deliberately concealed, their use by central banks is well documented.

An antitrust lawsuit filed in U.S. District Court in New Orleans implicated central and bullion banks and revealed another layer—and participant—in the precious metals manipulation scheme: gold mining companies.

In 2002, Blanchard & Company, a New Orleans coin and precious metals dealer, sued Canada-based miner Barrick Gold Corp. and JPMorgan Chase, a New York bullion bank, claiming the defendants rigged the gold price through the sale of gold borrowed from central banks. Blanchard alleged the defendants profited by trading derivative contracts and suppressing the gold price.

Barrick sought dismissal of the suit because the plaintiffs failed to include central banks, as well as other bullion banks and gold producers, as defendants. "As contracting parties, and as entities with a 'substantial interest' in all of the contracts at issue, the central banks, the absent bullion banks, and the absent gold producers are clearly 'indispensable' to this litigation," Barrick's attorneys argued.

The dismissal request also noted that U.S. law gives foreign central banks immunity from such litigation, and claimed foreign mining companies and bullion banks are beyond the federal court's jurisdiction.[26]

While the defendant's dismissal request was denied, the case was dismissed in 2005, avoiding disclosure of any misdeeds, after Barrick sued Blanchard for libel in Canada. Barrick received an apology and undisclosed cash settlement in its libel action.

Another participant in the gold leasing and swapping business is the Bank for International Settlements (BIS). Known as the central bank of central banks, the BIS has facilitated gold leases and swaps for decades, helping its 60 member banks intervene in foreign exchange markets. Based in Basel, Switzerland, the BIS touts its foreign exchange and gold services, including market interventions, in its reports and promotional materials.

A 1983 article in *Harper's Magazine* referred to BIS members as "the most exclusive, secretive, and powerful supranational club in the world."

"The club controls a bank with a $40 billion kitty in cash, government securities, and gold that constitutes about one-tenth of the world's available foreign exchange. The profits earned just from renting out its hoard of gold (second only to that of Fort Knox in value) are more than sufficient to pay for the expenses of the entire organization. And the unabashed purpose of its elite monthly meetings is to coordinate and, if possible, to control all monetary activities in the industrialized world," author Edward Jay Epstein wrote in the magazine's November 1983 issue.

Epstein, who interviewed BIS officials and was given a rare tour of BIS headquarters, added: "When the dollar came under attack in the 1960s, massive swaps of money and gold were arranged at the BIS for the defense of the U.S. currency."27

The magnitude and importance of central bank gold swaps and leases was a topic of discussion 14 years later during a meeting of the BIS's Gold and Foreign Exchange Market Committee.

"In May 1996, the market traded the equivalent of $3 billion of gold daily. Swap deals accounted for 75 percent of the volume," remarked Terry Smeeton, former head of the Bank of England's foreign exchange division, on April 7, 1997.

"Gold leasing was also a prominent piece of the market, whose growth central banks were very much a part of," said Smeeton, speaking to his banking counterparts from Belgium, Canada, France, Germany, Italy, Japan, the Netherlands, Sweden, Switzerland and the United States.

Smeeton added that central banks bore some responsibility for the gold leasing market since it was their activity that made the market possible to begin with.[28]

While central banks make leases and swaps possible, they're evasive about their application and function in financial markets. In fact, they use obscure—and deceptive—accounting practices to hide details about their loans and swaps. Confidentiality enhances the effectiveness of currency and gold market interventions, according to an IMF staff report dated March 10, 1999.

"Central bank officials," the report says, "indicated that they considered information on gold loans and swaps to be highly market-sensitive, in view of the limited number of participants in such transactions. Thus, they considered that . . . all monetary gold assets, including gold on loan or subject to swap agreements, [be disclosed] as a single data item."[29]

While central banks use creative accounting to camouflage their market interventions, swapping gold is perfectly legal, according to Virgil Mattingly, the Federal Reserve's former chief legal advisor. During a meeting of the Federal Reserve Open Market Committee in 1995, he suggested the law establishing the U.S. Treasury's Exchange Stabilization Fund (ESF) permits gold swaps.

"It's pretty clear that these ESF operations are authorized," said Mattingly, who retired in 2004 after 25 years as a member of the Federal Reserve's staff. "I don't think there is a legal problem in terms of the authority. The statute [establishing the ESF] is very broadly worded in terms of words like 'credit'—it has covered things like the gold swaps—and it confers broad authority."[30]

Originally funded with profit earned from gold surrendered by Americans during the Great Depression, the ESF was established by the Gold Reserve Act of 1934. The law permits intervention in gold and foreign exchange markets to support the U.S. dollar.

"For the purpose of stabilizing the exchange value of the dollar, the Secretary of the Treasury, with the approval of the President, directly or through such agencies as he may designate, is authorized, for the account of the fund established in this section, to deal in gold and foreign exchange and such other instruments of credit and securities as he may deem necessary to carry out the purpose of this section," reads a passage in the original law, amended in the late 1970s.

Today, the Federal Reserve, BIS, IMF and bullion banks serve as agents of the U.S. government. They sell, lease and swap metal, and trade financial derivatives to suppress gold and silver prices and protect the world's reserve currency. Yet, their methods and mechanisms remain largely shielded from public view and scrutiny.

Theories & Conspiracies

Even after slogging through the documentary evidence, much about precious metals price suppression remains a mystery. The complicated process and unfamiliar language are bewildering. Even longtime analysts ponder the extent and mechanics of market manipulation. Some dispute its existence all together. While the complex scheme is difficult to comprehend and ulterior motives hard to accept, confidentiality of gold and silver trading gives rise to speculation. Complexity and secrecy spawn both theories and conspiracies.

Economic and investment adviser Frank Veneroso estimates Western central banks may have depleted nearly half of their official gold reserves lending metal to bullion banks.

Veneroso explained the gold leasing process during GATA's African Gold Summit on May 10, 2001. He said central banks generate income by leasing gold to bullion banks. The bullion banks in turn sell the metal for cash and buy investments that earn a higher rate of return than the interest they pay on the borrowed gold. The problem is bullion banks can't return the gold unless they buy the metal back, so they hedge their risk by trading financial derivatives and manipulating the gold price.31

If Veneroso's theory is correct, central banks don't possess all of the gold they claim to have stored in their vaults, which would explain why they prefer to keep their gold leases and swaps confidential.

In rare remarks, Treasury Secretary Steve Mnuchin attempted to assure Americans about the nation's gold reserves after he visited the U.S. Bullion Depository in Fort Knox, Ky., on Aug. 21, 2017. "Glad gold is safe!" he declared via Twitter after touring the depository.32

Mnuchin also raised questions with statements he made to Bloomberg News. "We have approximately $200 billion of gold at Fort Knox," he said. "The last time anybody went in to see the gold, other than the Fort Knox people, was in 1974 when there was a congressional visit. And the last time it was counted was actually in 1953."33

With 4,583 tons of gold, Fort Knox holds the largest portion of the nation's gold reserves, though based on Mnuchin's comment the hoard hasn't been audited in 67 years. The U.S. Treasury's Office of Inspector General testified during a 2011 congressional hearing that audits of the nation's gold were conducted between 1975 and 1986, and again from 1993 to 2008. Regardless, conflicting information and lack of transparency inspire theories and conspiracies about the nation's gold holdings.

British economist Peter Warburton believes central banks encourage investment banks to use financial derivatives to suppress precious metal prices. That way they can bet against a rise in the price of gold and other commodities to mask inflation and the declining purchasing power of the dollar.

"Because their fate is intertwined with that of central banks, investment banks are willing participants in the battle against rising gold, oil and commodity prices," Warburton wrote in a 2001 essay titled "The Debasement of World Currency: It Is Inflation, But Not as We Know It."[34]

Silver market analyst Ted Butler contends silver is much more manipulated than gold or any other commodity. Butler claims JPMorgan Chase manipulates the silver price lower by trading COMEX futures contracts while simultaneously buying the metal. He estimates the bank has purchased 900 million ounces—or 27,990 tons—of silver since 2011, far more than was amassed by Nelson Bunker and W. Herbert Hunt, the Texas brothers fined $10 million each and banned from commodity trading in 1989 for conspiring to manipulate the silver market a decade earlier.

"You couldn't find anything more illegal or manipulative if you tried," Butler said during a "This Week in Money" interview on July 6, 2019.[35]

Central banks don't maintain large stockpiles of silver like they do gold. Central banks and national treasuries held an estimated 34,000 tons of gold in 2019, according to the World Gold Council.

Investment fund managers Paul Brodsky and Lee Quaintance speculate the purpose of price suppression is redistribution of the world's precious metal reserves. They suggest nations such as China and Russia want to amass as much metal as possible before prices are revalued higher against a new bullion-backed reserve currency, specifically the IMF's Special Drawing Rights (SDRs).

"Along these lines, global gold (and silver?) price suppression makes sense," the business partners wrote in a 2013 market letter titled "It's Time."[36]

Created by the IMF in 1969, SDRs are a monetary asset—a type of global currency—exchanged among central banks rather than individuals or corporations. They were created largely to decrease gold demand by reducing exchange of the metal for U.S. dollars.

"To be sure, excess dollar holdings of foreign central banks can now be used to purchase SDRs where formerly the only alternative to holding dollars was to demand gold from the United States and risk a monetary crisis," reads a declassified Central Intelligence Agency (CIA) memorandum titled "Special Drawing Rights: Paper Gold in Action." Marked "Confidential," the document is dated September 1970.[37]

Originally each SDR equaled 0.89 grams of gold. That value was abandoned in 1973 with the end of the international gold standard. Today, an SDR's value is based on a proportioned composite of the world's five leading currencies—the U.S. dollar, 42 percent; the euro, 31 percent; the Chinese renminbi, 11 percent; the Japanese yen and British pound, each 8 percent. The Chinese currency was added to the composite in 2016. The SDR's composition is evaluated every five years and is scheduled for review in 2021.

Chinese officials are aware of the gold price suppression scheme. China's government-controlled media has covered the topic.

"The United States and Europe have always suppressed the rising price of gold. They intend to weaken gold's function as an international reserve currency. They don't want to see other countries turning to gold reserves instead of the U.S. dollar or euro. Therefore, suppressing the price of gold is very beneficial for the United States in maintaining the U.S. dollar's role as the international reserve currency. China's increased gold reserves will thus act as a model and lead other countries toward reserving more gold. Large gold reserves are also beneficial in promoting the internationalization of the renminbi," reads a 2009 commentary in *Shijie Xinwenbao* (*World News Journal*), a Chinese newspaper.38

The translated article was included in a diplomatic cable sent from the U.S. embassy in Beijing to the U.S. State Department in Washington, D.C. Obtained by Wikileaks and released in 2011, the cable summarized stories in Chinese news media on April 28, 2009.

In 2009, China and Russia called for a new global currency to replace the U.S. dollar. China and Russia are buying gold and reducing their reliance on the dollar in foreign trade. Since 2010, both nations have increased their gold holdings, along with Ecuador, Hungary, India, Iraq, Kazakhstan, Mongolia, the Philippines, Poland, Qatar, Serbia, Turkey and the United Arab Emirates.

Other countries are bringing their gold reserves home. Since 2012, Austria, Belgium, Germany, the Netherlands, Hungary, Poland, Turkey and Venezuela have repatriated all or part of their gold from banks in London, New York and Paris, France.

In 2019, central banks around the world bought 650 tons of gold, the second highest total in 50 years and slightly less than the 656 tons they purchased in 2018.

Despite the renewed rush to gold, Americans are unaware of the trend unless they pay close attention to the financial news. U.S. politicians rarely mention gold and mainstream media typically avoid covering complicated and sensitive monetary matters. Maybe they don't want to alarm their constituents or concern their audiences. Perhaps they fear undermining the U.S. dollar or exposing a scheme with national and economic security implications. Whatever the reason, most Americans remain in the dark about the largest financial fraud in history.

Even when politicians inquire about gold, they often are dismissed, stonewalled or misled.

During a congressional hearing on July 13, 2011, Rep. Ron Paul (R-Texas) questioned Federal Reserve Chairman Ben Bernanke about gold, whose price at the time had risen to $1,580 an ounce.

When asked if gold is money, Bernanke replied "No," and referred to the precious metal as "an asset." When Paul inquired why central banks hold gold, Bernanke answered, "Well, it's tradition, long-term tradition."[39]

While Bernanke was correct about gold not being used as currency in everyday transactions, his claim that central banks hold gold merely for tradition sake was disingenuous, if not outright deceitful. Central banks wouldn't hoard and amass gold if it didn't have enduring value as money. They wouldn't lease and swap gold to suppress its price if it didn't compete with the U.S. dollar and other currencies. Secrecy and deception underlie precious metals manipulation and price suppression.

When Rep. Alex Mooney (R-W.Va.) began inquiring about the federal government's gold policy and market interventions in 2018, he received incomplete and questionable responses from the Federal Reserve and U.S. Treasury Department.

In an April 24, 2018 letter to Treasury Secretary Mnuchin and Federal Reserve Chairman Jerome Powell, Mooney posed six questions, including: "Does the U.S. government, through the Treasury Department, the Federal Reserve System, or any other agency or entity, transact in gold or gold derivatives either directly or through intermediaries? If so, what are those transactions and what are their objectives?"[40]

In their replies, Brad Bailey, acting assistant Treasury secretary, and Powell denied that the Treasury or central bank lease or swap precious metals or trade in their derivatives.[41] However, they didn't answer all of Mooney's questions, and some of their responses conflicted with documentary evidence and statements made by previous Federal Reserve and government officials.

For instance, in a Sept. 17, 2009 response to a Freedom of Information Act request for gold records by the Gold Anti-Trust Action Committee, former Federal Reserve Governor Kevin Warsh referred to "swap arrangements with foreign banks on behalf of the Federal Reserve System."[42]

Mooney, a member of the House Financial Services Committee and its Subcommittee on Monetary Policy and Trade, also questioned why a Commodity Futures Trading Commission (CFTC) investigation from 2008 to 2013 into silver market manipulation failed to find any wrongdoing when subsequent probes by the U.S. Department of Justice uncovered crimes committed during the same time period.

"Why did the commission fail to find the wrongdoing the Justice Department has confirmed and continues to investigate?" Mooney asked in a Feb. 5, 2019 letter to CFTC Chairman J. Christopher Giancarlo.43

Getting straight answers from federal regulators is a fool's errand. Investigations and enforcement actions are largely a facade to cover the U.S. government's own involvement in—and tacit approval of—market interventions.

Since 2014, more than a dozen precious metals traders have been charged with fraud and conspiracy. Most worked for some of the world's top investment banks and companies, including Bear Stearns, Deutsche Bank, JPMorgan, Merrill Lynch, Scotia Capital and UBS. Four pleaded guilty, three were convicted and one was acquitted. Others await trial.

On June 1, 2017, former Deutsche Bank metals trader David Liew pleaded guilty to manipulating gold, silver, platinum and palladium futures contracts between 2009 and 2012. The CFTC banned Liew from commodities trading the next day. As part of his plea, Liew admitted to conspiring with other metal traders and using an illegal tactic called spoofing.44 Spoofing involves placing buy or sell orders with intent to cancel them before completing the transactions. The goal is to manipulate prices and profit from the bogus trades.

On Sept. 25, 2020, former Deutsche Bank traders Cedric Chanu and James Vorley were convicted of wire fraud after Liew testified the men taught him how to spoof precious metal prices. Sentencing was scheduled Jan. 21, 2021, though attorneys for the convicted traders expressed plans to appeal their verdicts.

Former JPMorgan trader John Edmonds pleaded guilty on Oct. 9, 2018, to spoofing precious metals futures between 2009 and 2015. Edmonds reportedly learned illegal trading practices from his co-workers and used them with the knowledge and consent of supervisors.[45]

Edmonds' admission contradicted statements made by a JPMorgan executive six years earlier. During a CNBC interview on April 5, 2012, Blythe Masters, head of JPMorgan's global commodities division at the time, denied the bank manipulates precious metals. "That's not part of our business model," she said. "It would be wrong and we don't do it."[46]

Masters also contended JPMorgan only trades for its clients and has no stake whether a commodity price rises or falls. "Our business is a client-driven business, where we execute on behalf of clients to achieve their financial and risk management objectives," she said, leading some to wonder if the U.S. government or Federal Reserve is among the bank's clients.

On Sept. 16, 2019, federal prosecutors described JPMorgan's precious metals trading operations as a criminal enterprise and charged three of its traders under the Racketeer Influenced and Corrupt Organizations Act (RICO), a law often used against organized crime rings. Two months later, a former JPMorgan salesman was indicted in the criminal conspiracy.

"The defendants and others allegedly engaged in a massive, multiyear scheme to manipulate the market for precious metals futures contracts and defraud market participants," said Assistant Attorney General Brian A. Benczkowski in a press release.47

On Sept. 29, 2020, the Department of Justice announced a $920 million out-of-court settlement with JPMorgan after the nation's largest bank admitted its traders manipulated precious metals and U.S. Treasury markets between 2008 and 2016.

Some of the world's leading bullion banks and trading companies have been penalized for rigging precious metals. Fines and legal settlements totaling more than $1.1 billion have been collected from

Barclays, Bear Stearns, Deutsche Bank, HSBC, JPMorgan, Merrill Lynch, Morgan Stanley, Mitsubishi, Scotiabank and UBS since 2014.

The recent crackdown on market manipulation, however, isn't likely to end suppression of gold and silver prices. A handful of guilty pleas and convictions won't stop illegal trading practices, nor will financial penalties, which are a part of the cost of doing business for the world's biggest banks. The scope of the scheme is much bigger.

The Enduring Scheme

Suppression of gold and silver prices endures for a multitude of reasons, including apathy, concealment, ignorance and denial of the scheme.

The top reason is because the U.S. government and banks have a vital and mutually beneficial relationship. They rely on one another. The federal government won't allow the large banks to fail for fear of destabilizing or crashing the national and global economy. The $700 billion bank bailout of 2008 is proof of their interdependent and indispensable relationship.

In return, the banks, which are integrally linked in their own financial dealings, protect the U.S. dollar by lending and trading the currency while earning a profit. This ensures the almighty dollar remains the dominant global currency. Furthermore, the Federal Reserve creates the currency, helps finance the national debt and bolsters the entire financial system.

That's why the U.S. government indulges and defends the systemically important banks, including the central bank, even if they circumvent or violate the law. If one crucial bank were shuttered or fails, a chain reaction and financial crisis could ensue.

While federal authorities prosecute traders and impose fines for manipulating precious metals, the too-big-to-fail banks remain in business. The goal, it seems, is to feign enforcement rather than eradicate illegal trading and market manipulation. Otherwise, bank executives would be busted along with their law-breaking traders, and financial penalties would be stiff enough to break banks that operate criminal enterprises.

Illegal activity by the banking syndicate is unlikely to end until the kingpins are convicted and sent to prison, and fines aren't much of a deterrent as long as banks receive billion-dollar bailouts and penalties are a fraction of a bank's net worth. With assets of $2.7 trillion and a $36.4 billion profit in 2019, a $920 million settlement won't shutter—or shudder—JPMorgan.

Other factors contribute to the enduring scheme. Lack of knowledge about precious metals and the monetary system help perpetuate the plot, along with limited interest and scrutiny of market interventions and price suppression.

Most Americans know little about precious metals. Since gold and silver were removed from the monetary system decades ago, few are aware of their historic or current role. They don't know that foreign central banks are buying large quantities of gold or bringing their gold reserves home from overseas vaults. Other than in their jewelry, tableware and electronics, most Americans don't own gold or silver, or track their price. Indebted Americans can't afford much gold or silver.

Even those who can afford precious metals often are discouraged from buying and owning them. Some economists, financial commentators and investment advisers ridicule precious metals, referring to gold as a barbarous relic, pet rock or terrible investment.

Financial talk show host Dave Ramsey urges listeners to sell their gold and invest in mutual funds. "I do not own any gold nor am I buying any gold," Ramsey told his radio audience on Jan. 23, 2008. "It's a stupid investment."[48]

Billionaire investor Warren Buffett frequently bashes gold as an investment, arguing stocks have outperformed gold since he bought his first shares in 1942. "The magical metal was no match for the American mettle," wrote the Berkshire Hathaway CEO in a Feb. 23, 2019, letter to shareholders.[49]

The tide may be turning. Buffett's company invested $564 million in mega miner Barrick Gold in mid-2020.

Even though financial planners preach diversification, they seldom mention precious metals as part of a balanced investment portfolio. Some financial advisers say gold and silver prices are too volatile, which is true and by design to discourage demand. If precious metals are recommended, clients often are steered toward an exchange-traded fund or other financial product that may or may not be backed by physical gold or silver. If it's not, the investment contributes to the imaginary metal supply and price suppression scheme.

Lack of political inquiry and media attention also allows the scheme to persist.

Despite several attempts over the last decade, Congress has failed to pass legislation requiring an audit of the Federal Reserve, including its transactions with foreign central banks, governments and financial institutions. Such an audit could reveal gold leases, swaps or other mechanisms used to manipulate precious metals.

Similarly, Rep. Mooney hasn't gained much support since he introduced a bill in 2019 that would authorize an audit of the nation's gold reserves. A thorough, independent audit could determine if any of the vaulted gold has been sold or if encumbrances exist on the metal.

When it comes to financial accountability, most lawmakers shirk their responsibility. Based on their inaction, they prefer secrecy to transparency when it comes to the nation's gold holdings and precious metals manipulation.

Mainstream media are equally complicit and derelict in their duties. While news outlets may report the results of Justice Department and CFTC investigations, they rarely pursue details beyond those included in court records and government press releases. Even journalists provided with documentary evidence of a broader scheme refuse to delve deeper into precious metals manipulation. Since the massive fraud carries national and economic security implications, the topic likely is perceived as too sensitive for scrutiny or public disclosure. This helps explain why guest commentators who mention gold and silver price suppression during live broadcasts aren't invited back by the major financial news networks. The topic appears to be off limits on the public airwaves.

Whether due to biased financial advice, political concealment or media caution, most Americans remain uninformed about precious metals and the largest financial fraud in history.

Most precious metals mining executives remain mute on the subject as well, even though their livelihoods depend on profitable gold and silver production. Some speculate that their general silence is because the mining industry is government-regulated and mining companies obtain financing from banks that rig metal prices.

"Mining executives tend to shy away from things that could put a spotlight on them or their companies," explained Keith Neumeyer, CEO of First Majestic Silver Corp., during an interview on Jan. 13, 2017.

Neumeyer, whose Canadian company operates mines in Mexico, is one of the few mining executives who have spoken out about manipulation of gold and silver markets. "They are manipulated and have been for over 30 years," Neumeyer said during the Money Metals Exchange podcast.50

Skeptics, meanwhile, claim precious metals price suppression is a myth—or at least an abysmal failure—since gold and silver prices have risen substantially over the last two decades. Since 2000, the gold price has increased from $280 an ounce to a high of $2,000, while silver rose from $5 to as much as $50 an ounce.

Believers argue precious metal prices have not kept pace with the expanding money supply and overall price inflation. With global debt topping $250 trillion, they believe gold and silver remain greatly undervalued, proving that their prices are suppressed. If free markets prevail, some precious metal zealots claim gold could top $10,000 an ounce and silver could surpass $500.

Others insiders consider precious metals manipulation a fiction fabricated by gold and silver advocates and pitchmen.

During a podcast interview, precious metals expert Jeffrey Christian downplayed illegal trading in the commodities markets, calling it "petty manipulation." He described people who believe a larger plot exists to manipulate gold and silver prices as conspiracy theorists.

"We don't see grand conspiracies, and we see a tremendous amount of evidence that these grand conspiracies do not exist," Christian told Money Metals Exchange host Mike Gleason on Aug. 23, 2019.[51]

Christian didn't specify what evidence disproves a large, coordinated effort to suppress gold and silver prices. Those who examine the documentary evidence from the last 50 years discover as much conspiracy as theory.

The Fraud Will Fail

While the scheme endures, the fraud will fail. Suppression of precious metals won't last forever. Ultimately the law of supply and demand will prevail as purchases of physical gold—and possibly silver— overwhelm trading of imaginary metal. Either that, or a new gold-backed currency will emerge to replace the U.S. dollar.

Efforts to dethrone the dollar and restore gold to the monetary system already are underway. Central banks around the world are increasing gold purchases and returning their gold holdings from overseas vaults. This indicates declining confidence in the U.S. dollar and demonstrates faith in gold, which along with silver are the world's most trusted and time-tested money.

A few banking officials and investment tycoons have publicly acknowledged the enduring purpose and value of gold.

In 2010, former World Bank President Robert Zoellick proposed a new global monetary system. "The system should also consider employing gold as an international reference point of market expectations about inflation, deflation and future currency values," he wrote in a *Financial Times* article published Nov. 7, 2010. "Although textbooks may view gold as the old money, markets are using gold as an alternative monetary asset today."52

Billionaire Ray Dalio said people who don't own gold, don't know history and economics. "It's not sensible not to own gold," the hedge fund manager said during an interview at the Council on Foreign Relations on Sept. 12, 2012.53

"Gold has grown in importance over the course of history, first as a medium of payment, later as the bedrock of stability for the international monetary system," wrote Bundesbank President Jens Weidmann in the foreword to the 2019 book, "Germany's Gold."54

"For the first time in my life, I bought gold because it is a good hedge," said billionaire Sam Zell, chairman of Equity Group Investments, during a Bloomberg TV interview on Jan. 17, 2019. "Supply is shrinking and that is going to have a positive impact on the price."55

The Netherlands central bank called gold "the perfect piggy bank" and "the anchor of trust for the financial system" in an online report posted in April 2019. "If the system collapses, the gold stock can serve as a basis to build it up again. Gold bolsters confidence in the stability of the central bank's balance sheet and creates a sense of security."[56]

In 2017, the Basel Committee on Banking Supervision (BCBS), which sets standards for 28 of the world's central banks, reclassified gold bullion as a zero-risk asset equal to cash. As a result, more banks are likely to retain or increase their gold holdings as international regulatory reforms are phased in beginning Jan. 1, 2022.

While other nations, including China and Russia, are accumulating gold, the United States maintains a relatively stable stock, buying bullion primarily for coins the U.S. Mint produces and sells.

Due to its massive budget and trade deficits, the United States' position as an economic superpower is diminishing. The U.S. dollar's reign as the world's preeminent currency is fading. Like all dominant currencies of the past, including the Spanish dollar and British pound, the U.S. dollar eventually will be replaced. Suppression of precious metal prices only masks the currency's decline.

Even a JPMorgan employee questions the longevity of the U.S. dollar. In a July 10, 2019, article, Craig Cohen, a foreign exchange and commodities strategist, suggested the U.S. dollar could lose its status as the world's reserve currency.

"Given the persistent—and rising—deficits in the United States (in both fiscal and trade), we believe the U.S. dollar could become vulnerable to a loss of value relative to a more diversified basket of currencies, including gold," Cohen wrote in an article titled, "Is the Dollar's 'Exorbitant Privilege' Coming to an End?"[57]

Economist Robert Triffin predicted the dollar's demise 60 years ago. In his 1960 book, "Gold and the Dollar Crisis: The Future of Convertibility," Triffin warned currency creation would outpace gold production, triggering a monetary crisis and destroying the value of the dollar.[58]

"A fundamental reform of the international monetary system has long been overdue," Triffin testified during a congressional hearing in December 1960. "Its necessity and urgency are further highlighted today by the imminent threat to the once mighty U.S. dollar."[59]

Triffin made the statement more than a decade before President Nixon ended the international gold standard, which extended the life of the dollar as the world's reserve currency and necessitated the suppression of precious metals.

In his book, Triffin identified a dilemma for the nation that issues the world's dominant currency. To expand the global economy and supply other nations with sufficient currency for international trade, the United States must maintain a trade deficit, spending more on imports than it earns from the goods and services it exports. The paradox is an ever-larger quantity of currency in circulation, which depreciates its value and ensures its eventual destruction.

The overarching problem is the nation that issues the global reserve currency must serve conflicting interests. The United States must defend the dollar and support its domestic economy while fulfilling the needs of the world economy and financial system. The two objectives are at odds; for what benefits one, inevitably disadvantages the other.

This conundrum explains why issuing the world's top currency is both a blessing and a curse for the United States. Unconstrained currency creation and credit expansion promote economic growth, boost employment opportunities, increase bank and business profits, and allow Americans to consume more than they produce. And understandably, Americans don't want to lose the benefits of the blessing.

The blessing, however, comes with a high price, an inherent curse. Without precious metals backing to constrain currency creation, the U.S. dollar gradually is debased. Meanwhile, boundless credit expansion allows the nation's debts to grow so large they're unserviceable without inflating the money supply and destroying the remaining value of the currency. The dreaded and deadly curse is hard for the blessed to understand, much less accept.

Growing the global economy and ruling the world comes with other costs as well, including the loss of U.S. jobs to foreign competition and the need to maintain a strong overseas military presence. The loss of millions of manufacturing jobs, for instance, reduced potential exports, decreased middle-class wages and increased the need for government spending on social programs. In addition, the nation's armed forces are deployed around the globe to confront economic adversaries and security threats. Both warfare and welfare contribute to the nation's ballooning deficits and debt.

While the United States remains one of the wealthiest nations, it's also the most indebted. As trading partners tire of shouldering the nation's debt burden, the dollar's value will fall and precious metals suppression will fail. Countries and individuals will turn to gold and silver to preserve wealth.

The illusion of wealth created by currency and credit expansion underlies the largest financial fraud in history. Because the scheme was phased in over decades, few people noticed the deception. Ignorance was bliss as precious metals were demonetized, manipulated and denigrated while the nation's deficits and debt got bigger.

First, gold was coerced from American citizens and taken out of circulation. Second, silver was removed from the nation's coinage. Next, the international link between the dollar and gold was severed. Once that was accomplished, markets were rigged to suppress precious metals and convince the world the U.S. dollar was as good as gold and silver.

The truth is, it's not. If the dollar were as good as gold and silver, their prices wouldn't have to be rigged.

Afterword

Though business leaders and conservative politicians extol free-market capitalism, financial markets are far from free. Rigged precious metals markets are only part of the fraud. Banks and financial service companies also have been fined billions of dollars for rigging bond prices, interest rates and foreign exchange markets.

The entire financial system is fraught with flaws and fraud. It's built on an unlimited supply of increasingly worthless currency; infinite credit and bad investments; unregulated derivatives; massive deficits and debt; and routine market interventions.

If Wall Street banks get into financial trouble from reckless lending or risky investing, the Federal Reserve and U.S. government bail them out rather than shutting them down, perpetuating irresponsible behavior and enabling criminal activity among those that manipulate markets.

If the stock market plunges, the President's Working Group on Financial Markets, also known as the Plunge Protection Team, comes to the rescue with funds to stabilize the financial system. The team consists of the Treasury secretary and the chairpersons of the Federal

Reserve, Securities and Exchange Commission, and the Commodity Futures Trading Commission.

If foreign nations stop or reduce purchases of U.S. debt, the banks and Federal Reserve step in to buy it, keeping the bloated and profligate federal government afloat when it should cut spending or raise taxes to cover expenditures.

When the government borrows money to finance its enormous deficits and debt, the dollar is debased. To defend the dollar, precious metal prices are suppressed to conceal the currency's declining value.

Repeated interventions and market manipulation make it impossible to discover the appropriate price or true value of anything, be it a home, stock share or ounce of gold. The entire financial system becomes fraudulent without a foundation of sound, constitutional money.

Summary
Q&A

Who rigs precious metal markets?

The federal government and banks rig markets and suppress gold and silver prices. Market interventions occur via the U.S. Treasury's Exchange Stabilization Fund, the Federal Reserve, foreign central banks, bullion banks, the Bank for International Settlements (BIS) and the International Monetary Fund (IMF).

Why are precious metal prices manipulated and suppressed?

To support the U.S. dollar and its position as the world's reserve currency. Gold and silver are money, having served as mediums of exchange for 2,500 years. They compete with the U.S. dollar and act as a barometer on the declining value of paper and digital currencies.

Who benefits from price suppression and manipulation?

The federal government and banks benefit. Price suppression protects the U.S. dollar, bonds and other instruments that finance the nation's debt. Banks profit by trading and manipulating precious metals.

What evidence exists proving price rigging?

Government and bank documents, personal correspondence, and public testimony confirm manipulation and suppression of gold and silver prices. The Gold Anti-Trust Action Committee (GATA) maintains an archive of evidence at *www.gata.org*.

Where does price rigging occur?

Manipulation and price suppression occur in the precious metals markets, notably via trading in the London bullion market (LBMA) and the New York-based COMEX, the primary futures and options market for trading gold and silver.

When did price rigging begin?

Corrupt kings and authoritarian regimes have debased and manipulated currencies since ancient times. Modern price suppression efforts began in 1961 with formation of the London Gold Pool, comprised of the Federal Reserve and seven European central banks, to sell gold and limit its price to $35 an ounce.

How are precious metal prices manipulated and suppressed?

Central and bullion banks suppress prices by selling, swapping and leasing precious metals. Banks also use unregulated financial instruments called derivatives to create vast quantities of imaginary gold and silver and bet on their price. The imaginary metal exists only on paper or digitally, not in physical form. Trading imaginary metal in large volume allows banks to control the market for physical gold and silver and dictate their price. Traders also employ illegal practices such as spoofing, placing bogus buy and sell orders to manipulate metal prices for profit.

Who is responsible for policing and preventing market manipulation?

The Commodity Futures Trading Commission (CFTC) is charged with regulating precious metals markets and enforcing trading rules. The FBI conducts its own investigations into market manipulation and the U.S. Department of Justice is responsible for prosecuting violators.

Why aren't laws against market rigging enforced?

While more than a dozen traders and eight banks have been charged with manipulating precious metals markets since 2014, law enforcement and regulatory authorities aren't likely to stop it completely since the U.S government is a beneficiary—and coconspirator—of the scheme. Exposing the scheme could threaten economic stability and security by undermining the U.S. dollar.

Why do Americans allow price suppression to continue?

Due to its covertness and complexity, most Americans are unaware of precious metals price suppression. Politicians and the mass media largely avoid the issue. Presumably, they don't want to draw attention to the sensitive subject and risk undermining confidence in the dollar.

Will suppression of gold and silver prices ever end?

Price suppression will end when enough individuals and nations lose confidence in the U.S. dollar and put their faith in gold and silver. When trust is lost in devalued currencies, people turn to gold and silver to preserve wealth. Governments can do the same to restore confidence in collapsing currencies and monetary systems.

Why is gold and silver price rigging the largest financial fraud in history?

Gold and silver prices are rigged to defend the U.S. dollar. Since the dollar is the dominant currency in international trade, every foreign currency exchanged for dollars is rigged, along with the entire financial system. Global debt and the dollar supply have never been larger, so the financial fraud is the largest in history. The world was defrauded of sound money.

Endnotes

1. President Franklin D. Roosevelt's Executive Order 6102, April 5, 1933
www.fdrlibrary.marist.edu/_resources/images/eo/eo0001.pdf
2. President Roosevelt's fireside chat, May 7, 1933
https://millercenter.org/the-presidency/presidential-speeches/may-7-1933-fireside-chat-2-progress-during-first-two-months
3. Gold Reserve Act of 1934
www.loc.gov/law/help/statutes-at-large/73rd-congress/session-2/c73s2ch6.pdf
4. Silver Purchase Act of 1934
www.loc.gov/law/help/statutes-at-large/73rd-congress/session-2/c73s2ch674.pdf
5. Coinage Act of 1965
www.govinfo.gov/content/pkg/STATUTE-79/pdf/STATUTE-79-Pg254.pdf
6. President Lyndon B. Johnson's remarks, July 23, 1965
www.presidency.ucsb.edu/documents/remarks-the-signing-the-coinage-act
7. President Richard Nixon's televised address, Aug. 15, 1971
www.nixonfoundation.org/1971/08/the-challenge-of-peace-president-nixons-address-to-the-nation-on-a-new-economic-policy/
8. Public Law 93-373, signed by President Gerald Ford, Aug. 14, 1974
www.govinfo.gov/content/pkg/STATUTE-88/pdf/STATUTE-88-Pg445.pdf
9. Gold Bullion Act of 1985
www.govinfo.gov/content/pkg/STATUTE-99/pdf/STATUTE-99-Pg1177.pdf#page=1

10. Liberty Coin Act of 1985
www.govinfo.gov/content/pkg/STATUTE-99/pdf/STATUTE-99-Pg113.pdf#page=5
11. Federal Reserve memorandum, "U.S. Foreign Exchange Operations: Needs and Methods," April 5, 1961
https://fraser.stlouisfed.org/files/docs/historical/martin/23_06_19610405.pdf
12. Paul Volcker, "From Dollar Float to Inflation Fight," *The Nikkei Weekly*, Nov. 15, 2004
www.gata.org/files/VolckerMemoirs.pdf
13. Paul Volcker, *Changing Fortunes: The World's Money and The Threat to American Leadership*, (Crown, 1992), 232
14. William L. Silber, *Volcker: The Triumph of Persistence*, (Bloomsbury Press, 2012), 2
15. Valentin Schmid, "Paul Volcker: Gold Was the Enemy," *The Epoch Times*, March 26, 2015
www.theepochtimes.com/paul-volcker-gold-was-the-enemy_1299447.html
16. Jelle Zijlstra, *Dr. Jelle Zijlstra, Conversations and Writings*, (1979), 191
17. Jelle Zijlstra, *Per Slot Van Rekening*, (1992), 222
18. U.S. State Department transcript, April 25, 1974
https://history.state.gov/historicaldocuments/frus1969-76v31/d63
19. Arthur Burns letter to President Ford, June 3, 1975
www.gata.org/files/ArthurBurnsLetterToPresidentFord-June1975.pdf
20. Robert Barsky and Lawrence Summers, "Gibson's Paradox and the Gold Standard," *Journal of Political Economy*, (University of Chicago Press, June 1988)
21. Central Bank Gold Agreement, Sept. 26, 1999
www.gold.org/what-we-do/official-institutions/central-bank-gold-agreements/first-central-bank-gold-agreement
22. U.S. State Department telegram, Dec. 10, 1974
https://wikileaks.org/plusd/cables/1974LONDON16154_b.html

23. Federal Reserve Chairman Alan Greenspan testimony, July 24, 1998
www.federalreserve.gov/boarddocs/testimony/1998/1998072 4.htm

24. Commodity Futures Trading Commission hearing, March 25, 2010
www.cftc.gov/sites/default/files/idc/groups/public/@newsroo m/documents/file/metalmarkets_032510transcript.pdf

25. "Bullion Banking Explained," *Precious Metal Investor*, (CPM Group newsletter, February 2010)
www.gata.org/files/CPMGroup-BullionBankingExplained.pdf

26. Blanchard vs. Barrick, Dec. 3, 2002
www.gata.org/files/BarrickConfessionMotionToDismiss.pdf

27. Edward Jay Epstein, "Ruling the World of Money," *Harper's Magazine*, November 1983
www.edwardjayepstein.com/archived/moneyclub.htm

28. Gold and Foreign Exchange Committee meeting, April 7, 1997
www.gata.org/files/FedMemoG-10Gold&FXCommittee-4-29-1997.pdf

29. International Monetary Fund report, March 10, 1999
www.gata.org/files/IMFGoldDataMemo--3-10-1999.pdf

30. Federal Reserve Open Market Committee meeting, Jan. 31-Feb. 1, 1995
www.federalreserve.gov/monetarypolicy/files/FOMC199502 01meeting.pdf

31. Frank Veneroso presentation, GATA African Gold Summit, May 10, 2001
www.gata.org/node/5275

32. Treasury Secretary Steve Mnuchin tweet, Aug. 21, 2017
https://twitter.com/stevenmnuchin1/status/89972762459490 3040?lang=en

33. Saleha Moshin and Alister Bull, "Mnuchin's Fort Knox Quip: 'I Assume the Gold Is Still There,'" Bloomberg, Aug. 21, 2017

34. Peter Warburton, "The Debasement of World Currency: It Is Inflation, But Not as We Know It," April 9, 2001
www.gata.org/node/8303
35. Ted Butler, "This Week in Money" interview, July 6, 2019
www.howestreet.com/2019/07/06/this-week-in-money-190/
36. Paul Brodsky and Lee Quaintance, "It's Time," market letter, December 2013
www.gata.org/files/QBAMCOItsTime-12-2012.pdf
37. CIA memorandum, "Special Drawing Rights: Paper Gold in Action," September 1970
www.cia.gov/library/readingroom/docs/CIA-RDP85T00875R001600030133-1.pdf
38. "China increases its gold reserves in order to kill two birds with one stone," *Shijie Xinwenbao*, April 28, 2009
www.gata.org/files/USEmbassyBeijingCable-04-28-2009.txt
39. Federal Reserve Chairman Ben Bernanke testimony, July 13, 2011
www.youtube.com/watch?v=2NJnL10vZ1Y
40. Rep. Alex Mooney letter to U.S. Treasury Secretary Mnuchin and Federal Reserve Chairman Jerome Powell, April 24, 2018
www.gata.org/files/MooneyLetter-04-24-2018.pdf
41. U.S. Treasury and Federal Reserve letters, July 11 and July 12, 2018
www.gata.org/files/Treasury&FedResponsesToMooney-07-2018.pdf
42. Federal Reserve Governor Kevin Warsh letter, Sept. 17, 2009
www.gata.org/files/GATAFedResponse-09-17-2009.pdf
43. Rep. Mooney letter to CFTC Chairman J. Christopher Giancarlo, Feb. 5, 2019
www.gata.org/files/Mooney-Letter-CFTC-2-5-2019.pdf
44. United States vs. David Liew, May 24, 2017
www.justice.gov/criminal-fraud/file/972981/download

45. United States vs. John Edmonds, Oct. 9, 2018
www.justice.gov/criminal-fraud/file/1110956/download
46. Blythe Masters interview, April 5, 2012
www.cnbc.com/id/46808857
47. U.S. Department of Justice press release, Sept. 16, 2019
www.justice.gov/opa/pr/current-and-former-precious-metals-traders-charged-multi-year-market-manipulation
48. Dave Ramsey Show recording, Jan. 23, 2008
www.youtube.com/watch?v=S98_eMax9xo
49. Warren Buffet letter to Berkshire Hathaway shareholders, Feb. 23, 2019
www.berkshirehathaway.com/letters/2018ltr.pdf
50. Keith Neumeyer interview, Jan. 13, 2017
www.moneymetals.com/podcasts/2017/01/13/keith-neumeyer-first-majestic-000987
51. Jeffrey Christian interview, Aug. 23, 2019
www.moneymetals.com/podcasts/2019/08/23/higher-forecasting-for-gold-and-silver-prices-001850
52. Robert Zoellick, "The G20 must look beyond Bretton Woods," *Financial Times*, Nov. 7, 2010
www.ft.com/content/5bb39488-ea99-11df-b28d-00144feab49a
53. Ray Dalio interview, Sept. 12, 2012
www.cfr.org/event/conversation-ray-dalio
54. Carl-Ludwig Thiele, *Germany's Gold*, (Hirmer, 2019), foreword
55. Sam Zell interview, Bloomberg TV, Jan. 17, 2019
www.bloomberg.com/news/articles/2019-01-17/billionaire-zell-buys-gold-for-first-time-in-bet-on-tight-supply
56. De Nederlandsche Bank report, "DNB's Gold Stock," April 2019
www.dnb.nl/en/payments/goud/index.jsp#
57. Craig Cohen, "Is the Dollar's 'Exorbitant Privilege' Coming to an End?" July 10, 2019
https://privatebank.jpmorgan.com/gl/en/insights/investing/is-the-dollar-s-exorbitant-privilege-coming-to-an-end

58. Robert Triffin, *Gold and the Dollar Crisis: The Future of Convertibility*, (Yale University Press, 1960)
59. Robert Triffin testimony, "Current Economic Situation and Short-Run Outlook," Joint Economic Committee of Congress hearing, Dec. 7 and 8, 1960, 230

About the Author

A veteran newspaper reporter, magazine editor and writer, Stuart Englert also is the author of the "Paradox" novel trilogy, "Sold Out—How an American Magazine Lost Its Soul," and "Sweat & Sawdust: The Life and Legacy of Victor J. Hedinger."